A True Trash Tale About Plastics
With Parent/Teacher Guide

AUTHOR & ILLUSTRATOR
BRIDGET PARLATO

EDITOR, CINDER HYPKI

BE THE COOLEST! 1/2 OF
YOU AND YOUR FRIENDS CAN HAVE TONS OF FUN! NEW, FROM TONSOFFUN TOYS! DON'T J
LIMITED QUANTITIES AVAILABLE! SIZZLING SALES! INVENTORY LIQUIDATION! PRICES NEVER LOWER! GET BRIGHTIES! NOW W
EASY ONLINE SHOPPING! GET THE FASTET STUFF! NOW, WITH 50

Welcome all to Plastic Land!

On the surface
it might look quite grand,
but in this place
of plastic stuff
we don't know when
we've bought enough.
We never wonder
how stuff is made,
we only care
how low we've paid.
We rarely fix,
we rarely mend,
a scratch or tear
and it's the end.
And when we're asked
where our things go?
Most of us just say:
     "I don't know..."

Then we jam it all in plastic sacks
and put them out in piles and stacks
in every town, on every curb
in country, city and suburb
where mystery men we'll never meet
gather them up from street to street.

They load our
bagged-up
plastic feast
into a rolling
mechanical beast
that gobbles up
our trashy blend
with a hungry mouth
on it's great hind end.

The men then cling onto its side, the great mouth closes
and away they ride!

It's as if the trash just disappears
for days and weeks
and months and years!
We never give a second thought
to all the things we've used and bought—

the plastic wraps
and bags and lids,
the water bottles
for the kids,
the broken things
with which we've parted,
the packaging that
we've discarded.
Our minds just never
seem to clash
with thoughts of making
too much trash!

Without a thought we simply say, "Well, I'll just throw this thing away." Away from sight
AWAY?
AWAY?
AWAY?
AWAY?
AWAY?
AWAY?
AWAY?

The stuff we toss when we don't care
does not just turn into thin air.
The beast that gathers all our bags,
our wasted food, our wraps and rags
rolls right up to a great big hole,
one filled with trash, just like a bowl,
where all the stuff we throw away
gets tossed right in, day after day.

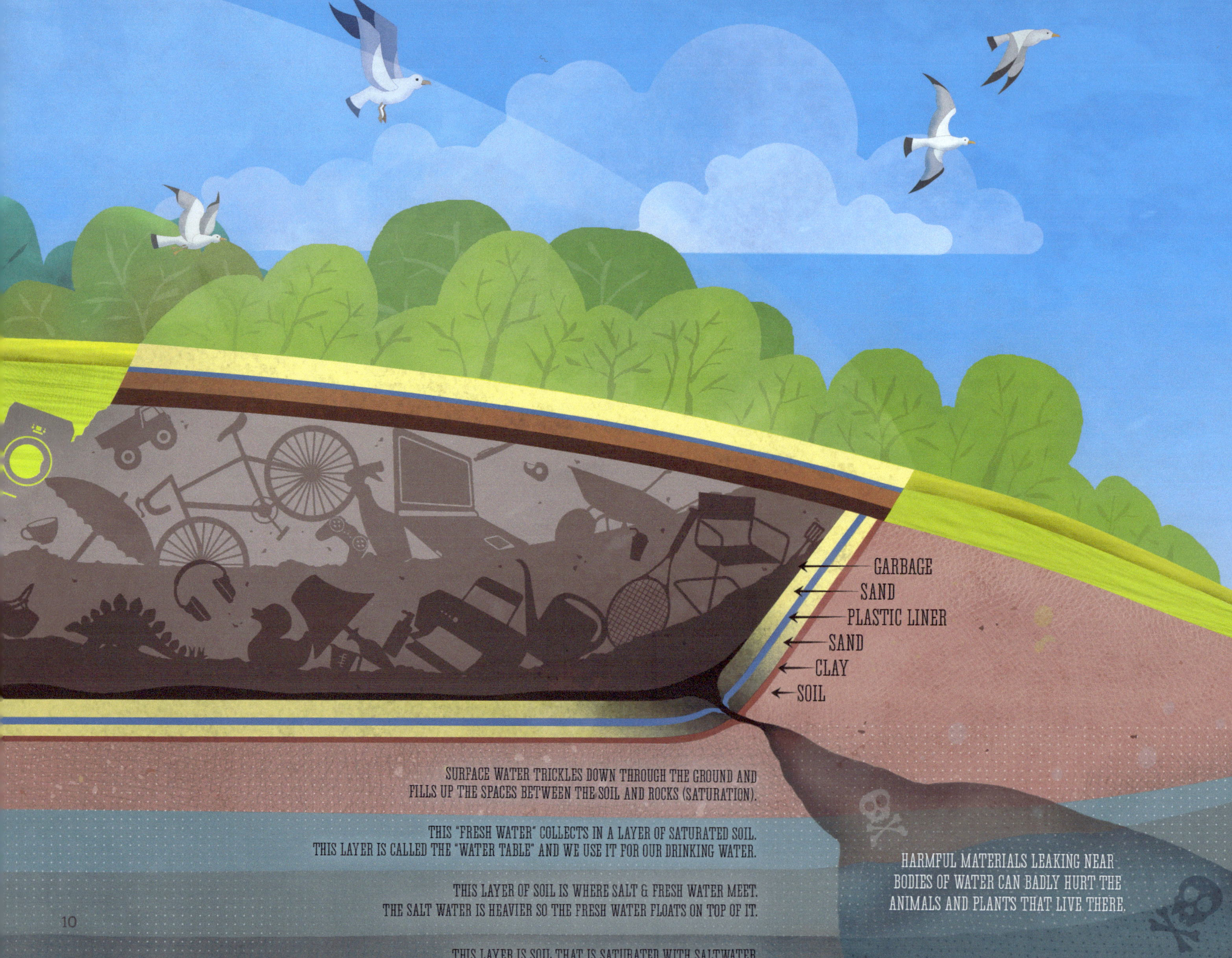

GARBAGE
SAND
PLASTIC LINER
SAND
CLAY
SOIL

SURFACE WATER TRICKLES DOWN THROUGH THE GROUND AND
FILLS UP THE SPACES BETWEEN THE SOIL AND ROCKS (SATURATION).

THIS "FRESH WATER" COLLECTS IN A LAYER OF SATURATED SOIL.
THIS LAYER IS CALLED THE "WATER TABLE" AND WE USE IT FOR OUR DRINKING WATER.

THIS LAYER OF SOIL IS WHERE SALT & FRESH WATER MEET.
THE SALT WATER IS HEAVIER SO THE FRESH WATER FLOATS ON TOP OF IT.

THIS LAYER IS SOIL THAT IS SATURATED WITH SALTWATER.

HARMFUL MATERIALS LEAKING NEAR
BODIES OF WATER CAN BADLY HURT THE
ANIMALS AND PLANTS THAT LIVE THERE.

We called them "dumps", but that sounds bad
to just dump all the things we've had.
But dump we do, into the holes,
then cover them all up with soil.
They're filled so high, they form big hills,
which we prefer to call "landfills".
Where we dump is still the same,
it's just called by a "nicer" name
(as if the land needs filling up
with all our broken, useless stuff)!

Most people do not understand
that trash that's piled up on land
creates a nasty ooze that seeps
into our waters, way down deep,
into streams, into our seas --
that nasty ooze can cause disease!

And just as bad as trash-filled craters,
we burn our stuff in incinerators.
They are places where our trash
is burned until it turns to ash.
While that may seem a good solution,
the smoke it makes is air pollution.

When plastic trash is burned to ashes,
its burning creates harmful gases.
These gases float into the sky
sending toxins way up high.

It's just no good for you and me
to keep polluting land and sea.
It's time we took much better care
of our water and our air.

So let's talk about
the way we live,
the stuff we buy,
the stuff we give.
From when we're born
to when we die,
every day
that we're alive,
a river of things
starts to flowing,
that grows with you
as you keep growing.
It widens, deepens,
and expands,
it's all that passes
through your hands.

Things you buy
when at the store,
things you don't use
anymore,
sneakers that have
run their mile,
clothes that have
gone out of style,
straws from drinks
at restaurants...
all your needs
and all your wants,
make plastic trash
that's here to stay,
it never really goes away.

It won't break down,
it doesn't rot
or decompose,
it's just forgot!
We should be told
to be afraid
of things that don't
biodegrade.
Our plastic trash
does not convert
from plastic things
back into dirt.
Instead our trash
forms cracks and splits,
and plastic turns
to plastic bits.
These microplastics
tend to flow
wherever wind
and water go.

They fill our oceans,
kill our whales!
Oh, I could tell you
awful tales
of furry beast
and feathered friend
who've met a painful,
tragic end,
their bellies full
of plastic scraps,
of plastic foam and bottle caps.
Even tiny one-celled beings,
the kind that you and I
aren't seeing,
though they've no eyes
or hands or feet,
they're so plugged up
that they can't eat!

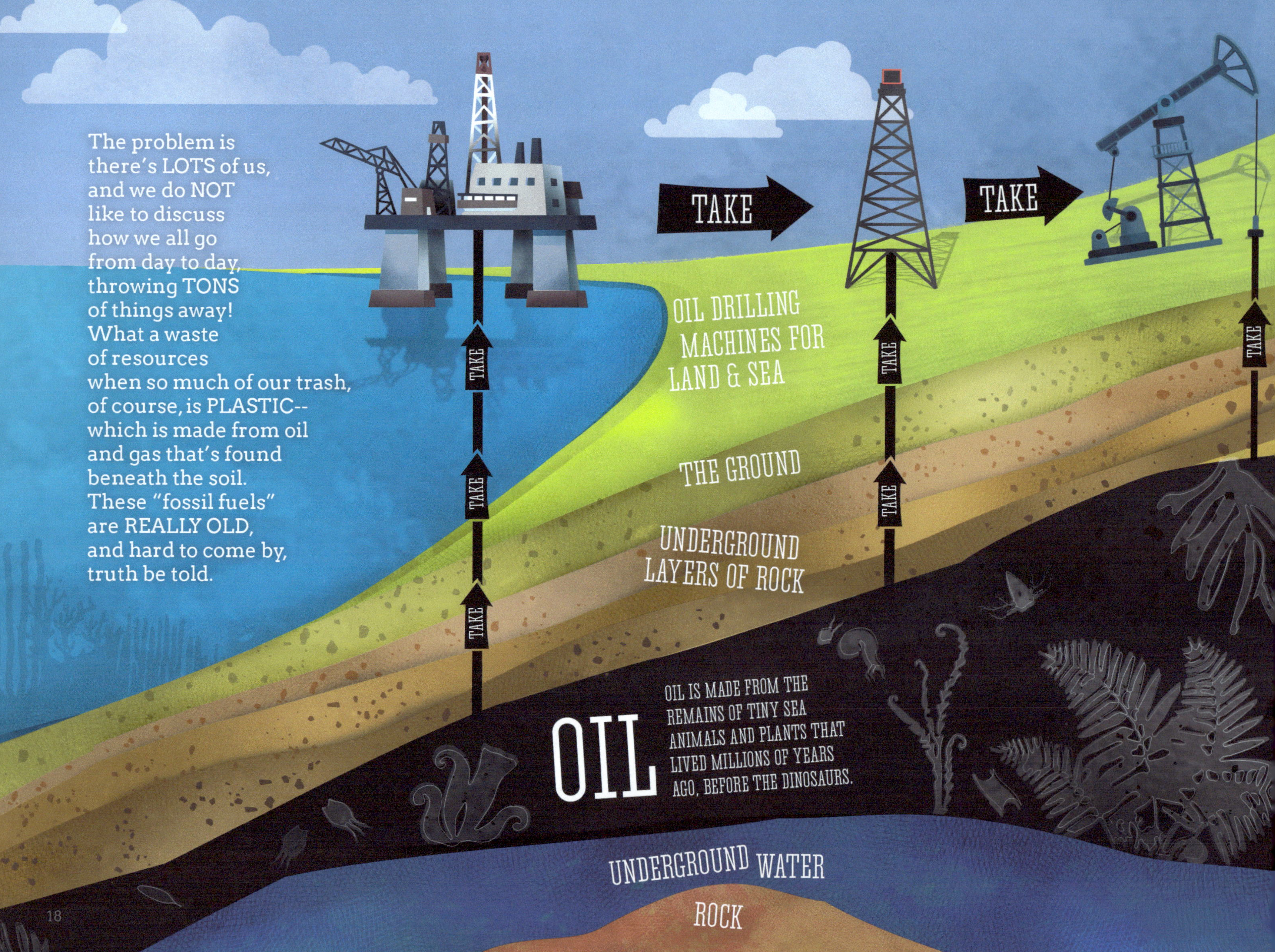

The problem is there's LOTS of us, and we do NOT like to discuss how we all go from day to day, throwing TONS of things away! What a waste of resources when so much of our trash, of course, is PLASTIC-- which is made from oil and gas that's found beneath the soil. These "fossil fuels" are REALLY OLD, and hard to come by, truth be told.

We drill and pump
and take, take, take,
and from these fuels
we make, make, make.
Forks and spoons and
plates and glasses,
pesticides
used on our grasses,
shampoos we use
to wash our hair,
and fabric for
our underwear.
It's in our soap
and toothpaste too,
all sorts of things
you use ON YOU!

Plastic things
are on our shelves,
in our closets,
on ourselves!
In hospitals
and stores and schools,
plastic toys and
plastic tools!
Useful, yes,
I do admit,
but when is there
too much of it?

Shouldn't we be limiting
making every little thing
from fuels that are
hard to get?
Perhaps some limits
could be set...

then plastic could
be wisely treated.
We would buy stuff
that is needed --

not just go for
something new,
or something that
looks good on you.

Yes, a new thing
makes you smile.
It feels good
for just a while.
But pretty soon
it's on the shelf
and then you're wanting
something else.
Being "new"
just doesn't last --
new things turn
to old things, fast.

We buy, we use, then in a flash,
we toss our things into the trash.

But if we all
could get in sync,
we could change
the way we think!
Then old and young
would not be faced
with all this stuff
we've turned to waste.
We could shop less,
buy less, toss less,
limit things
that we possess.
We could buy things
we'll reuse,
recycle things
we wisely choose,
vote for laws
that reduce litter,
make everything
around us glitter!

23

Better yet,
let's try to learn
that happy isn't
what you earn.
Happy isn't
in the "Thing",
happy is
experiencing!
It's talks and walks,
it's games and races,
it's trips we make
to other places.
It's meals we share
with those we love,
it's soaking up
the sun above.
It's learning something
that's exciting,
singing, dancing,
painting, writing!
It's working hard,
it's feeling proud,
it's smiling wide,
and laughing loud.

It's in the doing,
in the trying.
You won't find it
in the buying.
You want to undo
Plastic Land?
Just change your mind
and lend a hand...

These next few pages can help you and the children in your life become more aware of the problems created by plastics. When we all know more, everyone can make better choices for the planet!

Plastic

"Miracle"? Or disaster?

Hailed as a "miracle" invention in 1907, plastics became widely popular in the 1950's. It is an incredibly useful and versatile material that changed the lives of humans everywhere. Now over 100 years since its invention, we can see many reasons why it is not quite the "miracle" we thought it was.

The Good

It's cheap, it's versatile and plastic lasts a long, long time!

Plastic can be hard, soft, flexible, sturdy, see-through, colored, textured, smooth-- it can even LOOK like metal! But compared to other materials like metal or wood or glass, items made from plastic are often much cheaper to make: the cheaper it is to make an item, the less it costs.

With so many great qualities, it's no surprise that plastic is now used to make a bazillion things we see and use every day. And so many of those plastic items can be used for many, many years before they wear out and we have to replace them.

MANY, MANY YEARS?
That IS a long, long time! Good, right?

YES, BUT...

The Bad

Plastic lasts a long, long time!

Wait, wasn't that the good part?

YES, BUT...

Scientists have estimated that plastic can last for hundreds of years after we throw it away!

Hundreds. Of. Years.

THAT MEANS THAT EVERY PLASTIC THING YOU HAVE EVER USED IS STILL... SOMEWHERE, AND WILL BE THERE FOR A VERY, VERY, VERY LONG TIME.

People + Plastic

Creating long-term problems...

Most of us don't give plastic a thought, but

HUMANS MAKE HUNDREDS OF MILLIONS OF TONS OF PLASTIC EACH YEAR.

THAT'S TOO MUCH TRASH!

As time goes on, the number of humans on our planet has grown and that means the amount of plastic trash we've made has grown as well.

Our plastic trash is piling up, blowing around, getting into the food we eat, the water we drink, the animals we live with and into our own bodies.

Plastic is harming the land, the water, the animals, the bugs and birds -- our entire natural world -- including us.

Too Much Trash? But Trash Rots, Doesn't It?

Yes, *some* trash decomposes (rots). Some doesn't. It depends entirely on what **material** that trash is made from.

Materials - The Building Blocks

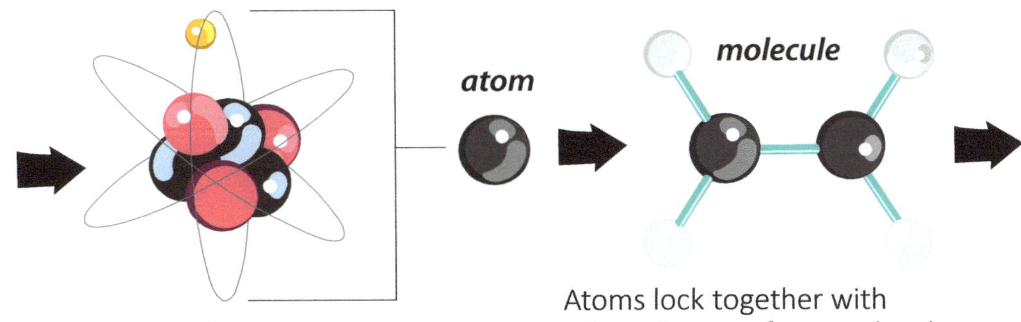

You, me, everything is made out of **atoms**. Think about an atom like a toy building block- only one that is so small you can't see it without a very strong microscope.

Drawing of an atom

Atoms lock together with other atoms to form molecules.

Different combinations of molecules make up different **materials** and we use materials to make our stuff.

What Rots and What Doesn't
Natural materials biodegrade (rot)

Natural or "Organic" Materials
Food, trees, plants, water, stone- are all made by and found in nature. These materials are called *"organic materials"*.

Biodegrading
Most organic materials break down little by little over time when left out in nature. This is due to the action of naturally occurring microorganisms such as bacteria and fungi. This process is known as "biodegrading".

If trash is biodegradable, it rots and turns into dirt.

Man-made materials
Man-made materials (also known as synthetic materials) are made by chemists and engineers.

They start as natural or organic materials but are transformed into other materials through chemical processes.

Plastics are man-made. They DON'T Biodegrade.
With exposure to light and air, plastic photodegrades. The plastic weakens, splits and breaks into tiny pieces called microplastics. These tiny plastic bits can move with water and air, causing pollution that is impossible to clean up.

Science experiments have estimated that the plastics we use will remain long after us and will never really rot.

Instead, the plastics we throw away will outlast us by hundreds and hundreds of years.

Plastic doesn't rot because of the way we make it

Almost all plastics are made from chemicals that come from fossil fuels.

What are fossil fuels?

Fossil fuels are found deep in the earth. They are formed from the remains of animals and plants that lived long ago. Over the earth's history, these remains were covered by layers of mud. Heat and pressure from these layers turned the remains into three things.

How Fossil Fuels Become Plastic

Drilling

Specialized machinery is used to drill deep into the ground and into the ocean floor to extract (take out) these fuels. This drilling creates a "well" from which the oil and gas are pumped up from the ground. Offshore, the wells are drilled from an oil platform. On land, the wells are drilled with an apparatus called an oil rig or drilling rig. Most modern wells can operate 24 hours a day. Then barge and tanker ships, pipelines, trucks and trains are used to transport the fossil fuels to refineries.

The Refinery

Before they can be made into plastics, fossil fuels need to be refined (purified) and processed. This produces a variety of products including ethane and propane.

The Cracker Plant

Ethane and propane are treated with high heat, in a process called "cracking". This changes their molecules. Once changed, ethane is called ethylene and propane is called propylene.

The molecules in ethylene and propylene are called monomers (individual atoms or small molecules). Monomers want to join up with other monomers in a chain. That chain is called a polymer.

Polymer Chains

Once polymer chains are formed, they are very long and very strong. Because polymers are not formed in the natural environment, there are no animals or microorganisms that have developed the ability to break them down. This is why these materials are not biodegradable.

Raw Plastic

Pellets, called "Nurdles," are formed from these polymers. The nurdles are then sent to plastic making factories.

The Plastic Factory

At a plastics factory, nurdles are melted into a thick liquid and more chemicals are added to make the liquid plastic hard. Dye is then added to give the plastic color. The liquid plastic is then poured into a mold (a container that gives a liquid a shape). The liquid cools down to harden into a solid plastic, producing a finished plastic product.

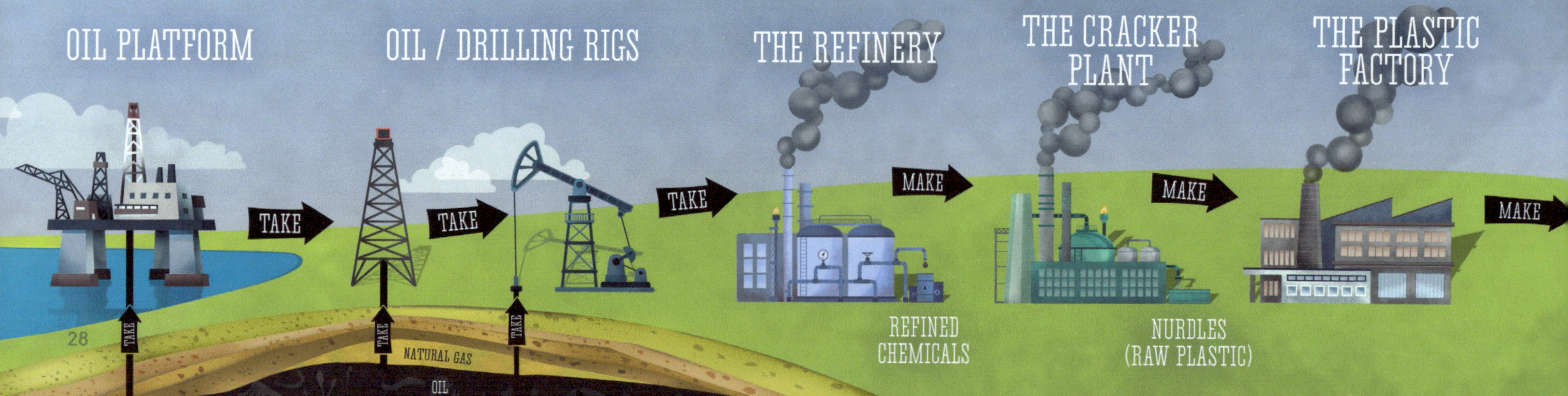

Plastic Types & Common Items

Polyethylene Terephthalate (PETE or PET)

Soda and water bottles, mouthwash bottles, peanut butter containers, salad dressing, vegetable oil containers

High-Density Polyethylene (HDPE)

Milk jugs, juice bottles, bleach/detergent/household clear bottles, shampoo bottles, some trash and shopping bags, motor oil bottles, cereal box liners

Polyvinyl Chloride (PVC)

Window cleaner and detergent bottles, shampoo bottles, clear food packaging, wire coverings, medical equipment, siding, windows, plumbing pipes

Low-Density Polyethylene (LDPE)

Squeezable bottles, bread/dry cleaning/shopping bags, tote bags, carpet

Polypropylene (PP)

Syrup bottles, ketchup bottles, straws, medicine bottles

Polystyrene or Styrofoam (PS)

Disposable plates and cups, meat trays, egg cartons, carry-out containers, aspirin bottles, compact disc cases

Miscellaneous plastics/Other

Polycarbonate, polylactide, acrylic, acrylonitrile butadiene, styrene, fiberglass, nylon, 3 and 5 gallon water bottles,"bullet-proof" materials, signs and displays, nylon, automotive parts, sunglass and eyeglass lenses, lighting fixtures, swim goggles and scuba masks, sporting equipment, hardhats, electronic and small appliance housings, toys (like legos), medical equiment... and much, much more!

"Throwing Away" Our Trash

"Away" is Somewhere.

- So ask yourself these questions:
- Do I know who takes out the trash in my house?
- Do I know what day the trash truck comes?
- Do I know where my trash goes on trash day?
- How many bags of trash do I/my family make each week?
- Was the trash from my past dumped near other people?
- Was my trash from the past dumped where animals are trying to live?
- Is my trash from the past polluting a place that was once clean and beautiful?

Where it goes...

Landfills

Most trash gets buried in a landfill, which is a fancy name for a large hole that gets filled with trash and covered with dirt. There are landfills near every town and every city.

At the landfill, our trash (in bags) is dumped, tightly compacted (pressed together) by heavy machinery and buried under clay and dirt. But for trash to decompose (rot), it needs air, light and moisture. Buried trash doesn't get exposed to these natural elements so even biodegradable trash can take decades to break down and become soil. Over time, landfills can leak poisons into the land and water that is around and beneath them.

Incinerators

Quite a lot of trash also gets burned in incinerators, which is a fancy name for a machine that burns waste. This skips the rotting process, but burning trash releases toxic (poisonous) gases and smoke into the air we breathe. This air pollution can be carried far and wide by the wind, causing illness for us and other living creatures.

Litter

People can be VERY careless about littering. Over time, the plastic we throw away or litter gets brittle, forms cracks and splits and breaks into microplastics that spread. Remember, micro means very small so imagine trying to clean up microplastics all over the world! And all those little teeny bits of plastic, STAY plastic for 50-1,000 years.

PLASTIC PROBLEMS

Plastic is Toxic

Unfortunately, many of the ingredients in plastic products are toxic. "Toxic" means that something is harmful or poisonous to living things.

Most plastics are made from oil-based chemicals and as plastic ages, it leaks some of these toxins. Humans and animals are exposed to a large variety of these toxins all along the plastic life cycle-- through inhalation, ingestion and direct skin contact.

Plastic and the chemicals it is made from have been found in our food and drinking water and scientists are only beginning to understand how these chemicals harm our bodies.

Plastics Create Pollution...

Plastic hasn't been around long. In just over 70 years, global plastic pollution jumped from two million tons (1950) to 348 million tons (2017), and is projected to double by 2040.

Because plastics don't rot, they are building up in landfills, in our streets and in our oceans where they eventually break up into microplastics.

Plastics can clog both natural and man-made water systems, causing floods and costing lots of money to fix and clean up.

Plastic Pollution is Costly!

Public trash/pollution cleanup is paid for with tax dollars. Taxes are fees that the government can collect from its citizens to pay for things that are needed by the public. So if you have a job, some of the money you make is collected. When you pay for a home or items at the store, some of the money you pay is collected too. This money is used to pay for schools, parks, roads, police, firefighters, soldiers, and many other public services that keep our towns and cities running smoothly.

If our tax dollars are paying for trash cleanup, there is less money to pay for the things we really need.

Plastic Pollution Hurts Animals...

It's Just Too Much...

Each year, people around the world create more than 7.5 million tons of litter and most of that litter is made of plastic. That's a LOT of plastic making it into the environment.

We understand what litter is, but animals don't. Both land and sea creatures often eat plastic because they mistake it for food. Food wrappers and carry-out containers that smell like food or often still have traces of food left on them are even more likely to get eaten.

In 2021, researchers found that 1,557 kinds of animals worldwide are now documented to have swallowed plastic. This research has been published in the famous and peer-reviewed journal Science.

What Happens...

Swallowed plastic fills the stomach and not surprisingly this reduces the feeling of hunger. Animals eat less, obtain less energy, and weaken. In worse cases, eating plastic can lead to intestinal blockage and internal injuries. Animals that accidentally eat plastic, suffer and often die as a result of it.

Abandoned nets, plastic ropes from fishing, packaging materials, plastic bags, six-pack beverage rings and other plastic trash can entangle animals. This kind of trash can even cause an animal to lose a fin or limb or it can get wrapped around the neck, causing strangulation. If an animal isn't able to move, hunt, or feed, it won't survive.

Microplastics are also harmful to animals. Microplastics absorb and concentrate pollutants from the surrounding environment. When animals eat or breathe in microplastics, they also take in the pollutants. These poisons can make it harder for the animals to have offspring and fight off illnesses, and can cause other long-term health problems.

Plastic pollution also destroys habitats for animals. As plastic waste accumulates, it disrupts the natural balance and functioning of ecosystems. For example, when plastic debris smothers corals in the ocean, the coral can't grow. Other animals who rely on coral beds for food and shelter also suffer.

In addition to marine life being harmed and killed by eating plastic, land-based mammals including elephants, hyenas, zebras, tigers, camels, cattle, dogs and other living things that have also consumed plastic waste resulting in unnecessary deaths.

and Humans, too.

We Are Part of the Animal Kingdom
We're never going to mistake a plastic bag for our dinner, but like animals, microplastics get in our bodies, carrying toxins with them. We too, can be harmed in many of the same ways that animals are.

Social Injustice
Plastics have also helped create a lot of inequality between people because of how and where plastic items are made.

Plastic things can be made very cheaply and are then shipped to us from all over the world using a lot of fossil fuel and creating pollution with each step. Not good...

So why make things so far away?

Businesses often make items in other countries because it's cheaper. The cost of labor (paying workers to make a product) is low and the laws protecting workers change from country to country. The clothing (fashion) industry is an example works this way.

Lots of clothing makers rely on people from countries like Bangladesh, Cambodia, India and China to create and deliver cheap clothing quickly to customers around the world. Of the 75 million people employed by the clothing industry, many are Black and Brown people and about 80% are women. These groups are frequently treated unfairly.

This is called *Social Injustice*. When people work very hard but are not paid enough or are not protected by the law, they can easily be treated poorly. They don't have access to important things like healthcare and education, they have very little time off and children often become workers at a young age.

It's important to protect children, treat all workers fairly and make sure they have enough resources to live healthy and happy lives.

STUDYING OUR STUFF

Plastic Challenges - What Can We Learn?

Every one of us uses and throws away plastic stuff every day. As we learned earlier, plastic doesn't biodegrade so each and every piece is adding up to ONE BIG MESS! But what if we ALL cut down on using plastics? Then our actions would add up as well-- but in a good way!

The following challenges can help us better understand how much plastic is in our lives. By understanding what our possessions are made from, we can make decisions to buy things that are friendlier to the planet, fix things instead of throwing them away and manage our trash systems better.

What's it made from? Materials & Properties

Properties

Here are some words that help describe the "properties" of a material.

- soft
- hard
- smooth
- rough
- transparent (see-through)
- opaque (not see-through)
- shiny
- dull
- rigid (stiff)
- flexible (bendable)
- solid
- malleable (formable)
- stretchy
- squashy
- waterproof
- absorbent
- fragile
- durable (long-lasting)
- heavy
- light

The following is a list of materials, and some of their properties

Metals
Common Items: silverware, pots and pans, scissors
Properties: hard, opaque, rigid (but might be flexible too!), often shiny, waterproof, durable, heavy or light (depending on the object), makes a ping sound when you hit it, often silver, grayish, gold or coppery in color.

Glass
Common Items: drinking glass, jar, window
Properties: hard, smooth, rigid, fragile, waterproof, transparent (much of the time)

Rubber
Common Items: rubber bands, balloons, surgical gloves, tires
Properties: hard or soft, opaque or semi-opaque, may be rigid or flexible

Textiles/fabric
Common Items: clothing, towels, blankets
Properties: soft, opaque or transparent, flexible, may be stretchy, squishy, waterproof or absorbent, light

Stone
Common Items: counter tops, gravel
Properties: hard, smooth or rough, opaque, rigid, durable

Wood
Common Items: furniture, paper, pencils
Properties: hard, opaque, rigid, has a "grain" texture

Composites
Common Items: reinforced concrete, plywood, fiberglass
Properties: hard, opaque, rigid

Plastic
Common Items: food container, plastic bag, toothbrush
Properties: hard or soft, opaque or transparent, rigid or flexible

Ceramics
Common Items: mug, bowl, plate
Properties: hard, smooth, opaque, rigid, fragile, waterproof

Challenge 1 - House Hunt

Look & List - Materials

The following challenges will help you understand what materials are used to make the items you use every day.

Look around your home or classroom and gather 20 things you use every day. Make a list of these items and write down what you think each item is made from. The materials & properties list on page 31 can help!

Use your senses. Look at the objects. Touch them. Pick them up if you can. Are they are light or heavy? Tap them with your fingernail or a pencil and listen to the sound the object makes. Does the object have a smell?

Have a parent or teacher look at your list and talk about your answers together. How many of the items you chose were made out of plastic?

Sample List

Item Name	Materials
Spoon	Metal (possibly plastic or a combination)
Chair	Wood, Fabric, metal (could be or include plastic)
Sneakers	Fabric, plastic

Helpful Hints -

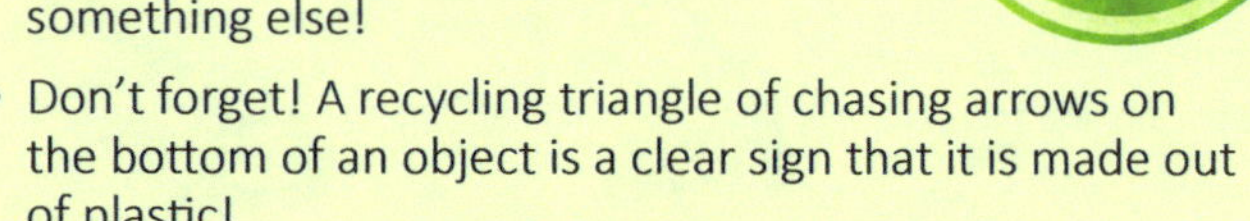

- Many things are made of a combination of materials.

- Some things may be made of plastic, but LOOK like they are made from something else!

- Don't forget! A recycling triangle of chasing arrows on the bottom of an object is a clear sign that it is made out of plastic!

- Using books or the internet together can help you learn more about the things you use everyday. To see how LOTS of stuff gets made, try this website, www.madehow.com

Challenge 3 Notes
Household Items

Item Name	Materials

Challenge 2 - Closet Count

Ever thought about what your clothes are made from? You'd probably be pretty surprised. Most of our clothing is plastic. For this challenge, let's take a deep dive into your closet to learn more. Understanding how our clothes are made and can help us make better decisions about our future purchases.

The word "clothing" comes from the word "cloth". Cloth is made from natural materials (cotton, wool, linen, flax, silk, alpaca, cashmere) or synthetic fabrics.

Long ago, people didn't own many clothes. Early pioneers in the 1800's had two or three sets of clothing, 1-2 for every day wear and one for special occasions. Thread, cloth and garments were mostly made at home.

By the 1900's, weaving and sewing machines made it possible for people to own perhaps 30-50 garments. However, clothing was only replaced every 2 years or as needed, *not* because the fashion trends changed.

People now often have hundreds of items of clothing and the average number of times each piece is worn before it is discarded **is only seven**. Clothing has become so cheap and available, it seems normal to throw it away.

To make cheap clothing, the fabrics used need to be cheap too. Cheap fabrics are made from non-renewable fossil fuels and are called synthetic fabrics; they are plastic! We wear these fabrics against our skin and they shed fibers when they are washed, sending microplastics and chemicals into our water. Cheap clothes are not well-made and end up in landfills after a very short lifespan, only to break down and become microplastics.

Look & List

You may have a LOT of clothes so start with choosing 20 of your favorite garments. Make sure to choose a variety of items: everyday clothes, swimsuits, sports uniforms, dance outfits, costumes, coats and shoes. Make a list of these items. Look at the labels and write down the names of the fabrics used to make them and where they were made.

Once you have made your list, compare the fabric names to the list of synthetic fibers and count how many of your favorites are made from or contain plastic fibers. You can also look at a map or globe to discover just how far your clothing traveled to get to you.

Remember, you have looked at only a few items of your own clothing. The rest of your family have closets full of plastic too. In fact, people all over the world are all wearing plastic clothing.

Sample List

Item Name	Materials	Where Was it Made? (check label)
Sweater	Acrylic	China
Winter Coat	Nylon & Polyfiber	Indonesia

What Labels Will Tell You

Labels can be found on the inside of a garment, on the back of the neck hole, on the inside seam, on waistbands and on the inside or bottom of your shoes.

- Labels tell you what your clothes are made out of.
- Labels tell you how to best care for your clothing so it lasts longer.
- Labels tell you where your clothes are made. Look for "Made in" China, Bangladesh, India, etc.

Quick Tip - If it glitters, stretches, has velcro, zips, buttons, laces, or clips, it usually contains plastic.

What Labels *Won't* Tell You

- 63% of the world's clothing is made from oil.
- The clothing industry is the second largest global polluter after the oil industry.
- The clothing industry uses a LOT of resources, *especially water.*
- How far your clothing was shipped (which leaves out the cost of the resources used to ship it).
- Whether the workers who created the clothing were treated fairly.
- Whether the workers who created the clothing were under-aged children.
- Most clothing gets thrown out, not repaired or donated to others who may need it.

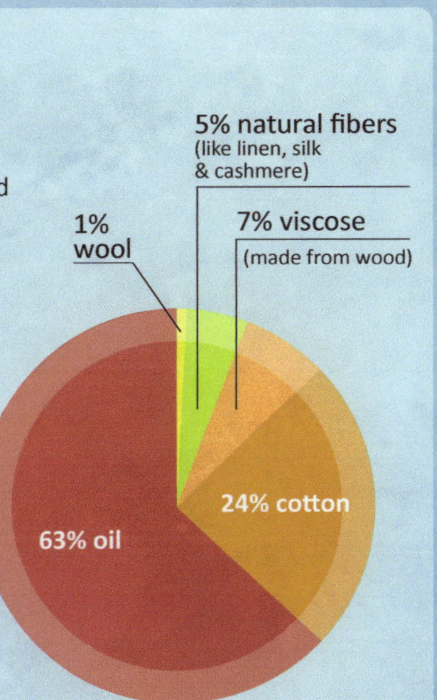

Challenge 3 Notes

Clothing

Item Name	Materials	Where Was it Made?

Synthetic Fibers

- Acetate
- Acrylic
- Aramid
- Arctic Fleece
- Avora
- Coolmax
- Cordura
- Dacron
- Darlexx
- DrySport
- Dyneema
- Elastane
- Elastic
- Fleece
- Gore-tex
- Kevlar
- Lurex
- Lycra
- Microfiber
- Modacrylic
- Nano Care
- Neoprene
- Nomex
- Nylon
- Olefin
- Polartec
- Polyester
- Rayon
- Rhinotek
- Schoeller
- Solarmax
- Spandex
- Supplex,
- Synthetic fur
- Synthetic leather
- Synthetic suede
- Tactel
- Terelyne
- Toughtek
- Vinylon
- Zylon

It's a Lot, But There's More...

Because plastic is so versatile, it can be hard to tell what is made from plastic and what is not-- kind of makes it hard to know just how much plastic you use every day.

The following challenges will help you identify plastic use in your bathroom, kitchen and personal possessions. Ask a parent or teacher to help you identify the materials if you need to. You may need to use the internet to confirm your answers.

Challenge 3 - Bathroom

Look & List

Write down 20 items in your bathroom and list the material/s they are made from. Are they made from plastic? Or have parts that are plastic? Are or were they packaged in plastic?

Hidden plastics: Band-aids, cotton swabs, sunscreen, disposable wipes, some toothpaste and skin care products, cosmetics. Look for these ingredients: polyethylene (PE), polymethyl methacrylate (PMMA), nylon, polyethylene terephthalate (PET) and polypropylene (PP).

Challenge 4 - Kitchen

Look & List

Write down 20 items in your cupboards, pantry, refrigerator, freezer and under the sink. Are they made from plastic? Or have parts that are plastic? Are or were they packaged in plastic?

Hidden plastics: plastic lining on beverage and food cans, bottle caps, drink cartons (milk and other), the inside of the lids on glass jars, some tea bags, to-go cups for coffee, small appliances, cookware, storage containers, etc.

Challenge 5 - Personal Stuff

Look & List

Write down 20 items like toys, games, electronic and gaming equipment, backpacks, and sporting equipment. List whether they are made of, packaged in or contain plastic (or all three). These items may not be clearly labeled and may have plastic parts that are not noticeable at first.

Hidden plastics: Sport balls, glitter, chewing gum, crafting supplies, school and office supplies, etc.

Remember, homes across the world that have the same plastic stuff you have and it all becomes trash.

Bathroom Items

Item Name	Made from plastic? Have parts that are plastic? Packaged in plastic?

Kitchen Items

Item Name	Made from plastic? Have parts that are plastic? Packaged in plastic?

Personal Items

Item Name	Made from plastic? Have parts that are plastic? Packaged in plastic?

SIMPLE SOLUTIONS
to the Plastic Problem

- Buy less
- Take care of what you have
- Fix things
- Cut down waste
- Dispose of things responsibly
- Protect & clean up the environment

Every Day Actions that Battle the Plastic Problem

Before You Buy...

Shopping Tips

Now that you've taken a good look at the plastic in your life, discuss what you have learned with others. The actions below can help cut down on plastic waste and plastic pollution. Sharing them with others **is** caring for the planet!

Say No to the Unnecessary. Shopping can feel good, but that good feeling quickly wears off so we go shopping again, often over-spending and accumulating a lot of unused stuff. When we buy things, the factories make more. When we say NO to more stuff by not spending our money on it, factories won't make as much. That reduces the plastic items that end up in the trash.

The Quest for Quality. Higher quality items may cost more than cheaply-made versions, but your purchase will last longer, preventing you from having to buy that item again and again, making trash along the way.

Refuse One-use. Any single-use plastic item sticks around for hundreds of years. Every time you order a single-use drink, that's three pieces of plastic (cup, lid, straw). Pay attention to what is one-use and say no if it is a want and not an absolute need. Ninety percent of the plastic items in our daily lives are used once and then thrown away: grocery bags, plastic wrap, "disposable" eating utensils (forks, spoons, knives), straws, coffee-cup lids. It's pretty easy to use reusable versions instead.

Take Back the Tap. Stop buying bottled water. Each year, close to 20 billion plastic bottles are tossed in the trash. Carry a reusable bottle with you.

Cook more. Not only is it healthier, but making your own meals doesn't involve takeout containers or to-go bags.

Trim-Down Your Take-Out. For those times when you do order in or have left-overs to bring home, tell the restaurant you don't need any plastic eating utensils, extra napkins or a million packets of sauce. If you can, pass on the plastic bag too!

Bring Your Bags. Reusable bags can be kept in places like your family car, purses, brief cases, backpacks and next to your front door so one is always handy.

Purchase items secondhand. Thrift stores, neighborhood garage sales, or online postings are good places to find items that have been previously owned, but still have a lot of "life" in them. You'll cut down on packaging that becomes trash and save yourself a few bucks, too.

Write to product manufacturers. Though we can make a difference through our own habits, large businesses can make a much bigger difference if they change their products. If you believe a company could make products in a better way, make your voice heard. Write a letter asking them to change the way they make things and choose to buy more earth-friendly products.

Research shows that **reusing just 10%** of the plastic products we buy would reduce the amount of plastic waste reaching the ocean **by HALF 50%**

Give It a Longer Life

Of the 100 billion garments produced each year, 92 million tons of clothing end up in landfills. More than 60% of that waste is made from synthetic fabric. The longer your clothes last, the less you need to buy. The better you care for them, the less microplastic fibers they shed into the environment. AND the less money you spend.

Here are a few tips...

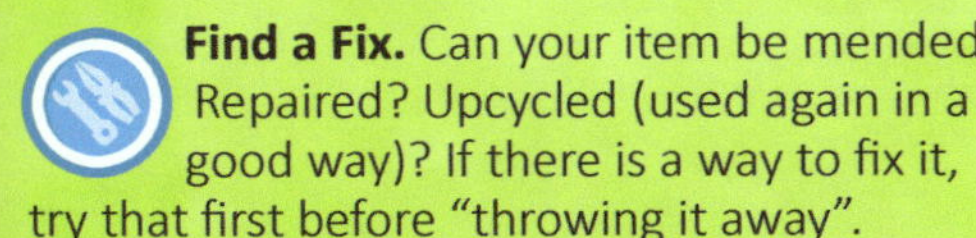

Find a Fix. Can your item be mended? Repaired? Upcycled (used again in a good way)? If there is a way to fix it, try that first before "throwing it away".

Washing Clothes. The first rule of washing is don't do it. If it's not soiled, you can air it out or steam it to give it a little bit of "extra life" for a few more days. Your clothes will last longer and not shed fibers so it's better for the environment if you can prolong the gaps between washes.

Cold-Water Wash. Wash your clothes on cold, at 20 or even 30 degrees less than what the care label tells you. Cold water is less harsh on fabric, and also will prevent shrinkage. Turn anything dark inside-out to prevent fading.

Skip the Dryer. Air dry your clothes to make them last longer. If you don't have the space to air-dry all your clothes, air-dry anything that stretches. Heat destroys stretchy clothing.

Donate/Swap. What do you do with a piece of clothing when you are tired of it? Is it still in good condition? There are many organizations that accept used clothing and goods. Or have a neighborhood clothing swap where you trade things you no longer want or use.

Good Taste go to Waste!

The United States throws out more food than *any other country in the world*: almost *40 percent of the entire US food supply*. That's around 325 pounds of waste per person. In fact, *food takes up the most space in US landfills*. And almost ALL that food comes wrapped in plastic.

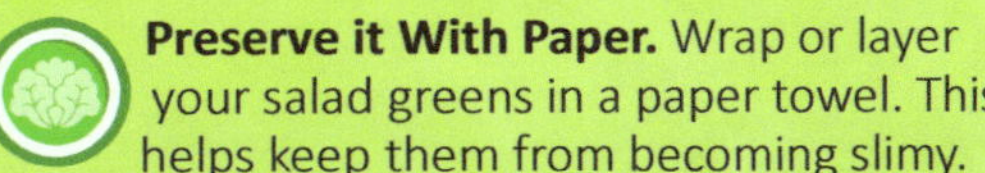

Stand it on its head. Store items upside down. After opening items packaged in jars or cartons (salsa, spaghetti sauce, cottage cheese), store them upside down to keep mold at bay. Just be sure the lid is on tightly first.

Preserve it With Paper. Wrap or layer your salad greens in a paper towel. This helps keep them from becoming slimy.

Hands off! Touching cheese directly can transfer bacteria from your hands to the cheese, which can cause it to spoil faster. Keep the wrapper on blocks of cheese when you cut them.

Your Freezer is Your Friend. Freeze food such as bread, sliced fruit, meat, or leftovers that you know won't be eaten in time. Label with the contents and dates. Store your flour in the freezer. This helps keep it fresh and avoid any icky bug infestations.

Buy in Bulk. By shopping from local farmers markets and buying in bulk, you'll be supporting local farmers, getting fresher ingredients and reducing packaging waste. Local food isn't shipped as far or refrigerated in transit so local farmers often can rely on less packaging. Don't forget to bring your bags!

Net Those Veggies! Don't buy veggies packaged on foam trays covered by plastic film, net your veggies! Net bags for veggies can be bought in stores, on the internet, used, washed and hung up to dry for years of reuse.

Trash Tips

Recycling Reduces: More recycling = less plastic trash. Reducing the amount of plastic you buy, use and throw away is even better.

Watch the Weather: Recycling that is put on the curb in paper bags or cardboard boxes can become plastic litter when the weather is bad. Instead, use a sturdy bin with a lid for recycling (using plastic bags for your recycling can harm the recycling machinery).

Lids Limit Litter: Trash and recycling items blow and flow with wind and water. A bin with a tight-fitting lid keeps trash and recycling from becoming plastic litter.

Not at Night: If your trash is not in a can overnight, rats and/or other animals WILL consider it dinner. Chewed bags create plastic street litter and critters come back to look for more.

Say No to Overflow: Whether using your trash can, your recycling bin, or a street corner can, stop at the top. Trash doesn't fit? Find a new can for it. Trash on top of or beside a street-corner can becomes plastic street litter.

Rapidly Report: Check to see if your city or town has a phone number or an app you can use to report problems you discover. Report trash issues and dumping when you discover them and be specific about the location and problem so that the city will have the proper tools and solutions to clean it up.

Keep it Neat from Step to Street: You are the FIRST and BEST defense against litter and plastic pollution. If everyone took 10 minutes to clean up an area around their home or school, the world would be cleaner and safer for us and the other living creatures we share it with.

OUR CHOICES ADD UP!
so let's make good ones!

Helpful Reference Websites

BBC Earth (bbcearth.com)

The Center for Science in the Public Interest (cspinet.org/)

Commons (thecommons.earth)

Condor Ferries (condorferries.co.uk/)

Consumer Reports (consumerreports.org/)

Earth. org (earth.org)

Ecology Center (ologycenter.org)

Fibershed (fibershed.org/)

How It's Made (YouTube channel)

How Products are Made (madehow.com)

How Stuff Works (howstuffworks.com/)

The Natural Resources Defense Council (nrdc.org/)

PBS Learning Media (mpt.pbslearningmedia.org/)

Plastic Soup Foundation (plasticsoupfoundation.org)

Scientific American (scientificamerican.com/)

Shell Oil (shell.us)

Sierra Club (sierraclub.org/)

Society for Conservation Biology (conbio.org)

Surfrider Foundation (surfrider.org/))

This is Plastics (thisisplastics.com/)

"Someday, I'm going to write a book." *Me, age 7 or 8...*

Written and illustrated by Bridget I. Parlato, B.Spoken Studio

Eco-Artist and Author, Bridget Parlato lives in Baltimore, MD where she creates and designs work that encourages people to take better care of our planet.

With Thanks

To Jeff Trueman, who reminds me how creative I am when the wolves stop by. His hard work grants me the gift of time.

To Cinder Hypki, neighbor, friend, fellow artist and editor. Her honest opinions and worthwhile suggestions have been truly helpful.

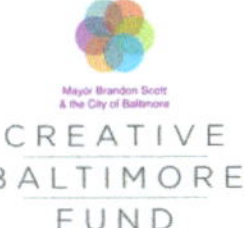

To Baltimore Mayor Brandon Scott and the Baltimore Creative Fund for assistance with funding the illustration of this book.

ISBN 979-8-9903699-0-0